RATS

THE ESSENTIAL GUIDE TO OWNERSHIP & CARE FOR YOUR PET

Kate H. Pellham

© 2015

DISCLAIMER

Edition v1.0 (15.11.27)

Table of Contents

Chapter 1: Introduction to Pet Rats

Rats have been living side by side with humans for centuries, and though you may not see them very often in your daily life, you're likely at least familiar with the species. Rats are rodents, and have close genetic ties to mice and hamsters. Forty percent of all modern mammals are rodents, and though there are hundreds of distinct species, all rodents share a jaw and tooth structure that allows them to gnaw through a surprising array of materials. The name rodent, in fact, is derived from the Latin word *rodere*—to gnaw.

All domestic rats are descendants of brown rats (*Rattus norvegicus*), which spread throughout Europe and North America in the 18th century. These are different than the black rat (*Rattus rattus*) that reached Europe in the 12th century aboard sea-faring vessels. Brown rats are generally larger and more aggressive. Though both species are prolific climbers, if they share an urban habitat, brown rats will live in basements and foundations, while black rats will inhabit the upper floors and attics. In rural areas, brown rats will live in burrows in the summer, moving into homes or barns during the winter. Though all rats are omnivores, brown rats in general prefer a diet with more animal protein than black rats, who are largely vegetarian.

Domestic rats range in length from 12-18 inches and weigh around 10-17 ounces (about 300-500 grams), with males generally larger than females. They have a round body that tapers toward the neck and a tail that's shorter than the length of the body. While there are no true breeds of rat, there are some mutations and variants, including tail-less rats (Manx), hairless rats (Sphinx), and dumbo rats, whose ears are larger. A standard rat has agouti fur, meaning the hairs are color-banded, usually grayish blue close to the skin, yellow in the middle, and black at the tip. The fur of the belly is typically white. Some rats are solid colored in shades of black, brown, gray, and yellow. Common fur patterns include hooded (darker head and shoulders with a white body), Irish (white except the chest and legs), and Berkshire (solid bodies with white chest, belly, legs, and tail). There are also albino rats, which lack pigment entirely and are white with pink eyes, and Rex-coated rats, who have curly coats. Rats bred for specific non-standard traits are known as fancy rats, and tend to cost a bit more to buy.

Rats are generally nocturnal feeders and are most active at night, though they wake and sleep sporadically throughout the day. They can climb anything that gives them a toe-hold, even if it's completely vertical, and shimmy up drain pipes by bracing their backs against a parallel wall. They are extremely agile, climbing over clotheslines and telephone wires with ease. Though they do enjoy animal flesh, rats are scavengers rather than hunters, and aside from the occasional bug they're not known to attack or catch live food. They live communally in the wild and have a distinct social hierarchy, often consisting of one alpha male with a harem of females and some subservient, smaller males rounding out the pack.

Human beings have been keeping rats since the 1800s. They were initially rounded up for sport, put into a ring for dogs to kill while people watch and place bets. The more unusual-looking rats—like albinos, or those with patterned coats—were often spared and kept as pets, leading to the first rat shows in the 19th century. This is likely a factor in the relatively large proportion of albinos in the modern domestic rat population. Eventually, their intelligence and availability led scientists to use them for medical research, a practice which has continued since the 1890s.

Rats are very scent-driven. That's how they identify each other, and they do the same with humans when they're kept in captivity. They also hear very well and are not fond of loud, sharp noises. Rats are adapted to environments with dim lighting. Small hairs along their bodies and the whiskers on their face can be used to feel their way around. Rats generally have very poor eyesight. They don't see colors and can distinguish very few details. They do have excellent depth perception and can accurately jump long distances. If they fall, they have a cat-like ability to land on their feet.

In the wild, female rats will keep a variety of nests scattered around her territory, just in case she needs to hide in a hurry. These nests will have bedding material and small stashes of food. They're also known to hoard objects, especially things that are shiny—bottle caps, coins, and jewelry are often found in a rat's hidden stashes. The entrances to these nests are often very small to prevent predators from following. Rats can move through remarkably tight spaces, and are capable of fitting through an opening no larger than a quarter.

Rats as pets

In a way, rats combine the best attributes of small animals and larger pets. Their care is relatively simple, on par with that of a hamster or gerbil, but they're far more intelligent an affectionate than these smaller animals. They can be trained to do basic tricks, like a dog can and show their keepers the kind of independent-minded love you could expect from a pet cat. Because they've been used in medical research for so long a lot is known about their nutrition, and you can provide them a complete diet of pre-made food. Though it's best to spend time with a pet rat every day, they can also fend for themselves during the occasional busy week. They readily adapt to a wide variety of schedules. Because they require relatively little space (2 cubic feet of floor space for a pair of rats) they are excellent pets for apartment-dwellers and the supplies you need to care for them are relatively inexpensive, both initially and long-term. Though it's a good idea to take them for an initial health checkup, rats don't need any shots or vaccinations, and you don't need a license to keep them.

There are a few things you should keep in mind before you take on the responsibility of any pet. Because they have fur, rats will likely trigger reactions in people who have allergies to other pet dander. Rat urine can have a strong odor. Regular cage cleaning is necessary to keep the smell under control. While rats aren't usually very noisy animals, they do get most active at night and will be up eating, running on their wheel, and climbing around their cage. Consider whether this noise at night will be an issue before bringing rats into your house. A rat's average lifespan is 2-3 years, but with proper care they can live as long as 5 years. You should be prepared to care for a rat for the entirety of its life before you commit yourself to its care.

One important thing to keep in mind is that rats should always be kept at least in pairs. Rats live in colonies in the wild and have an instinctual desire to groom and play with others of their own kind that even the most attentive keeper can't satisfy. Keeping a rat alone is like keeping a human in solitary confinement. He might not die, but he certain won't be as happy. Solitary rats tend to develop behavioral problems, either getting introverted and defensive or clingy and neurotic, and have even been known to self-mutilate. Some people mistakenly believe that keeping a rat by itself will make it more likely to bond to the humans in the house. In fact the opposite is true. A rat with a companion will be better socialized and ultimately friendlier than a solitary animal. It doesn't take significantly more time or money to care for two rats than it does for one, but it's something to keep in mind when you're considering whether rats are the pets for you.

Wild vs. domestic rats

A lot of people are dubious about rats as pets because they have a reputation for spreading disease. When it comes to wild rats, this reputation is not entirely un-earned, though it is misleading. The most wide-spread example of rats spreading disease was in Medieval Europe, when the black rats traveling on ships contributed to the spread of the Bubonic Plague. The real reason the plague spread so quickly was the same thing that drew the rats—poor sanitation practices that promoted bacterial growth. When they're living alongside humans, rats are frequent visitors to garbage dumps, so while it's not fair to blame the Bubonic Plague on rats, wild rats can be carriers of diseases picked up in their foraging.

Domestic rats, however, are a far cry from their wild counterparts. They spend their entire life in comfortable enclosures, far from any garbage dumps, and provided you keep their enclosure clean they are no more likely to carry illnesses than your average dog or cat. Behaviorally, domestic rats are less aggressive and more receptive to handling than wild rats. Especially if you buy your pets from a breeder, you can guarantee they've been selectively bred to produce the friendliest and most adaptable rats, and are handled from an early age to get them used to people. It is never a good idea to cage a rat from the woods, the street, or even from your basement. These wild animals aren't used to cages and will not like being trapped, and they may be carrying parasites or illnesses that you don't want to expose yourself to. Let wild animals be wild, and keep your pets captive-bred.

Cost of rat ownership

Your initial budget for setting up a rat cage will probably be in the neighborhood of $100-$200, depending on what kind of cage and supplies you buy. Rats themselves are very inexpensive, between $15 and $30 per animal. They're much cheaper at a pet store, often around $5-$10, and you may be able to adopt one for free or close to it from a rescue organization. Most of your initial expense is going to be for the cage. A basic model will cost around $40. Larger and more elaborate designs can run upwards of $250. How much you need to spend will depend on how many rats you plan on keeping and how elaborate you want the cage to be. You should also factor an initial vet checkup into your starting budget. Most visits will cost around $35-$50 per visit, depending on your vet.

In terms of ongoing costs, they're fairly minimal. You can expect to spend about $20 a month on food and bedding, plus the costs of any extra toys or cage furnishings you want to pick up along the way. Veterinary care for a rat can cost as much as that for a cat or dog, if they encounter a serious health problem as they age, so you should be prepared for that expense if something should happen.

Rats and children

Rats are excellent pets for children. Their care is relatively simple and straightforward, and is both easy and safe for a child to do. Rats are naturally inquisitive and affectionate and kids can have a lot of fun during playtime, although playtime should be supervised by an adult until the child is out of grade school. They also make excellent classroom pets, since they're awake sporadically throughout the day but fairly self-sufficient and won't be too distracting. Because rats can live to be as old as five, you should make sure your child is serious about wanting to own a pet before you go out shopping. Rats are also not a great pet to keep in a child's bedroom—or any bedroom, for that matter—because of the amount of noise they make during the night. If you're buying pet rats for a child, consider buying males. Female rats are generally more active, and are more likely to wriggle away from a child during playtime.

Rats and other pets

Cats and dogs are natural predators of rats, and generally speaking it is not safe to allow them to interact. Individual animals may be exceptions to this rule; take an honest assessment of your cat or dog's personality before introducing them to the rat. This doesn't mean you can't keep pet rats if you own a cat, but you will likely need to take extra precautions to keep the cat away from the cage.

On the other end of the spectrum, rats will often instinctually attack smaller rodents, like mice, gerbils, and hamsters. This is a territorial issue, to keep interlopers from their turf in the wild. Don't allow shared playtime between rats and smaller mammals or you risk injury to one or both.

Gender and colonies

Both genders make great pets, but they do have distinct personality differences. Both male and female rats are friendly with their keepers and adapt easily to being petted, carried, or fed by hand. Though male rats are larger and stronger, they also tend to be a bit calmer and more docile. They move more slowly and are less likely to try at (or succeed in) escape attempts. Female rats, on the other hand, are far more curious and love to explore. They're the rats that will wriggle out of your hands—not because they don't like you, but because they don't want to sit still. Female rats are especially energetic when they're in heat, which happens for 12 hours about once every five days. Females in heat have been known to undo latches on cage doors and shove weights off the top of glass aquaria. Female rats can be more interesting to watch, but they are a handful. Interestingly, females tend to do better at rat shows, and are the more popular gender as pets.

Over the age of about 3 weeks, it's very easy to tell male and female rats apart. Males have two rather large testicles hanging underneath their tail; females do not. Though both genders of rat may develop tumors later in life, females frequently develop what are known as mammary tumors, which affect their inner thighs, chest, and internal organs. These tumors can be invasive and costly to remove. They can be largely prevented by spaying females when they're young.

You should never house intact animals of opposite genders in the same enclosure. That is to say you should keep females with females and males with males. Even if they're neutered, males will generally get along better with other male cage-mates, though you can safely keep a neutered male in an enclosure with females. Even if you plan on breeding, you don't want to keep the parents together full-time. A female rat is capable of reproducing year round, and can get pregnant again even while she's still nursing a litter. Overbreeding puts enormous strain on the female rat's body, leading to serious health issues. If you plan on breeding your rats, you'll need a minimum of four animals to start—the breeding pair and a same-gendered cage-mate for each of them.

Finding the right animal

The most important thing when you're shopping

for pet rats is to make sure you buy healthy animals.

A rat's coat should be sleek, shiny, and unbroken.

Don't buy a rat whose coat looks ruffled, puffed-up, or

has bald patches. Check the animal's face and avoid

buying a rat with discharge coming from its nose,

eyes, or ears. Watch the rat interacting with its

environment. It should walk with an even gait, no limps or favored limbs, and the head should be moving naturally, not listing or tilted to one side. You also want to look at the condition of the cage in which it's being kept. Make sure it doesn't look overcrowded and that it's relatively clean. There should be fresh food and water available. If you can see any droppings, they should be hard and black or dark brown, with a defined shape, not amorphous, runny, or oddly-colored.

It's recommended to adopt your rats when they're around 4-5 weeks old. By 10 weeks old, they begin to establish their dominance hierarchies, so you'll find it easiest to bond with your new pets—and easiest to introduce them to other animals—if you purchase them within this sweet spot. This is especially important if you're buying the animals from a pet store, where they may not have been handled as often and will be difficult to make accustomed to human touch after that 10-week mark. If you can find a pair of same-sex litter mates, that is ideal. These animals will already have a natural bond, and since they're comfortable with each other, it'll make it easier for them to bond with you, too.

Buying your animal

It is strongly recommended to buy pet rats straight from a reputable breeder. Rats that have been bred to be pets are handled daily from the time they're very young, so they're used to people and your bonding process will be much faster. Most fancy rats are selectively bred not only for their unique coats and features, but also for their personalities—they are the offspring of the least aggressive males, the ones who have responded best to their human keepers, and the cumulative effects of this careful breeding make for much friendlier, more affectionate rats. Breeders will also give you a wider range of choices when it comes to appearance and personality than a pet store.

A good breeder will keep records of lineage on their rats dating back several generations. They will have rats separated by gender, and sick or nursing animals in quarantine cages—and all of those cages will be clean. You should watch the breeder handle her rats. They should come to her willingly, at least for the most part, and seem well-accustomed to her touch. You should be wary of any breeder that seems more concerned with making the sale than with the proper care of the animals. Rat breeders are not especially hard to find (you can search online, or check out the extensive list published by the Rat Fan Club; there's a link in the back of the book). If you have a bad feeling about a breeder or her rats, don't be afraid to look elsewhere.

You can find rats at most pet stores, often for a fraction of the price you can find them at a breeder.

The reason they're so cheap is that they're not intended to be kept as pets. These are feeder rats, whether they're labeled as such or not and are being sold as dinner for pets like snakes, birds, and carnivorous lizards. Unlike fancy rats, they are not hand-gentled from the time they are young. They are often kept in mixed-gender enclosures—it may sound callous, but these rats were not intended to live long enough to be concerned about the health risks of inbreeding. You should avoid these animals if you're looking for pets, and only buy rats from a pet store if they're fancy rats from a known breeder.

Another option is to rescue or adopt a pet, whether through your local humane society or from a newspaper ad or online listing. Adopting a pet can be a gamble. Rescued rats may have chronic health issues due to poor diet and neglect. It is always more difficult to bond with an older rat, but it could be especially hard to build trust if they were mistreated by humans in the past. On the other hand, adopted rats may come from a loving home that's re-homing the animals because of a life change. Examine the rats closely for the same signs of ill health you'd look for at a breeder, and if you go this route just know the bonding process may take a little longer. While all new pets should be taken for a vet checkup, it is especially important to do with adopted animals.

Chapter 2: Cage and Supplies

It's a good idea to have everything you need for your new pet rats before you buy the animals. Rats are masterful escape artists, capable of fitting through openings as small as a quarter, and their first instinct when they're afraid or stressed is to escape in search of somewhere to hide. A cage that's not ready to go when your new rats come home is likely to result in long night of searching your home for your frightened animals—a stressful endeavor for both you and your new pet.

As you can probably assume from the warning above, security is key when it comes to your rat enclosures. This is of special concern if you have does. Female rats in heat have an uncanny level of determination to escape their confines and find mates, even if there're no male rats in your home. Regardless of gender, pet rats have been known to figure out most door latch systems, and many keepers use combination locks on their cage lids and doors to prevent this.

A rat's powerful jaws are capable of chewing through anything made of plastic or wood. Because of that, these materials should be avoided in the cage's construction, also including any platforms or ramps that you install in the cage. Aside from the risk of escape and falling injury, rats that chew on plastic furnishings can swallow pieces of the plastic, causing intestinal distress or blockage. Wood is also a bad construction material because it can absorb urine, leading to elevated ammonia levels inside the enclosure. Wood should be provided to help your rats keep their teeth filed down, but anything made of wood or other paper byproducts—like cardboard—should not be expected to last long.

Since rats need to be kept at least in pairs and are fairly active animals, they require significantly more space than a hamster or gerbil. The minimum healthy size for a rat enclosure is a floor space of 12" by 24" and a height of at least 12". This goes for a single rat as well as a pair (though, as has been stated previously, it is not recommended to keep a solitary rat long-term). As with most animals, larger is better if you can manage it. For bigger colonies, a good rule of thumb is a cubic foot of space per rat. Since rats are excellent climbers, multi-level enclosures, like those designed for ferrets, can help increase the overall usable space for your pets without taking up an entire room of your house. Some large breeding operations keep colonies of 10 individuals or more; if you have a very large colony, make sure there's plenty of space and a variety of nesting options. Multiple food locations and water bottles will also be helpful.

Provided you have two or more rats, you should also plan on keeping a secondary enclosure on hand.

This cage can be smaller than your colony's cage (though you should make sure it's got at least two feet of floor space, the same as you would provide for a single rat). This secondary enclosure can serve as a nursing area if one of your pets gets sick or injured, and can also be used to transport your animals to the vet, or to quarantine new arrivals should you buy more rats down the line. The secondary enclosure can be simpler than the main cage, but should still contain, at a minimum, a food dish, a water bottle, a nesting box or hiding area, and some kind of litter, bedding, or liner.

Because they do get so bonded with their keepers, some people want to keep rats as a free-range pet, letting them run throughout the entire house or apartment. This practice isn't recommended. Possible escape is less the issue here than the potential for a rat to do damage to itself. Rats are naturally curious and love both exploring and chewing. The wide array of electronics, appliances, and other dangers available in any human home are simply too numerous to make. It's asking for trouble to let a rat run free in a house or apartment unless it's under your direct supervision.

There are two main recommended styles for rat enclosures: coated wire cages, or glass or Plexiglas aquaria. Each option has its own advantages and disadvantages that are discussed below.

Coated wire cages

This is the most popular enclosure style among rat keepers. Wire cages can be more easily converted into multi-level enclosures by attaching ramps, platforms, and climbing ropes to the sides of the cage. The under-cage litter pan design of many of these cages keeps the rat from walking through its own waste, and the open sides provide excellent ventilation, important to preventing ammonia build-up. If you're going with a wire cage, make sure the openings between the bars are no more than ½" apart. Also make sure that you buy a powder-coated or plastic-coated design. Certain acids in urine corrode metal over time, releasing the zinc in galvanized steel cages, which can be toxic if consumed.

If the cage has a floor of open wire mesh, you'll want to buy something to cover it. Walking on open wire can cause a condition known as Bumblefoot, where hard calluses develop on the pads of the rat's feet and then become infected. A piece of solid Plexiglas can work for this, though if you still want to utilize the under-cage litter tray, you can instead use a piece of plastic mesh needlepoint canvas from your local craft store. The bedding you put on top should keep your rats from gnawing on it too much. Keep a spare piece or two on hand to swap out while you're cleaning. Don't use wood, cardboard, or any other paper product as the flooring.

Multi-level ferret cages are popular designs for rat colonies. These models can be pricy but their tower construction makes them great space-savers, while still giving your animals lots of space to play. Rabbit cages can also work well if the spaces between the bars aren't too wide. Some keepers find bird cages to be excellent options because of the amount of vertical space they offer. Cages designed for hamsters or gerbils will typically be too small, but in truth it doesn't matter what animal species the cage is marketed for provided it gives your rats a healthy amount of space and can't be gnawed or wriggled out of. In all of these cases, make sure any ramps or platforms made of open wire mesh are covered with pieces of Plexiglas, cloth, or metal to protect your rats' feet.

Glass aquaria

A glass aquarium with a 20-gallon or larger capacity can make a fine habitat for a pair of rats. Since the sides are solid, ventilation is a greater concern, and solid-sided cages need to be cleaned about twice as often as open-sided designs. The temperature and humidity inside a glass enclosure will also generally be higher, so you'll have to watch your rats carefully in warm weather for signs of overheating. You may also need to get creative with installing cage furnishings, like a water bottle or climbing rope. A glass aquarium is also going to be heavier than a wire cage with the same interior volume and is more likely to break if dropped or struck. On the plus side, the solid walls of a glass aquarium do provide more security if you have other pets in the house, like cats and dogs, that may pester the rats.

Some colorful acrylic cages are sold in the small animal section for use with rats, guinea pigs, or smaller rodents. Many of these are too small to be suitable for a rat, but if they're of adequate size and provide decent ventilation, they could be suitable enclosures. Keep in mind, however, that even if the rats aren't able to gnaw through the acrylic, their nails may scratch it, making it difficult to see through clearly. Acrylic cages in general have the same drawbacks and advantages as glass aquaria, except that they're lighter weight and more resistant to shattering.

Cage placement

Rats in the wild often share their environment with humans, and the temperature range that they prefer is very similar to a human being's—between 65° and 80°F. Drastic temperature changes can weaken the animal's immune system and make the more likely to develop health problems, so when you're considering where to put your rat cage you should avoid placing it directly in front of any windows, where sunlight filtering through the glass could overheat the enclosure. Similarly, avoid drafty areas, or placing them directly under or over any heating and cooling vents, to prevent sudden shifts in air temperature.

Rats like a relative humidity between 40 and 70%. Again, this shouldn't be difficult to maintain in a human environment except in the winter, when the air is generally drier. An environment that's too dry can lead to respiratory and skin problems. A humidifier in the room where the rat's cage lives during the winter months may be helpful if you notice your pets scratching or sneezing.

Dim to moderate light is best for rat cages. Rats are accustomed to living in fairly dark environments and too much light can damage their eyes. This is especially true of albino rats, whose eyes lack the pigment necessary to block out radiation. The light put off by incandescent bulbs in a normal home shouldn't be too much for a rat; fluorescent bulbs and very bright natural sunlight are more likely to be problems. If the room where the cage lives is especially bright, you may want to cover part of it with a blanket or towel. Portable screens and curtains can also be used to make the rat's area of the room dimmer.

Rats don't sleep on the same schedule as a human. They prefer to sleep in small increments throughout the day, meaning they'll be up and active around the clock. In the wild, they do most of their foraging and exploring at night, and will be especially active and playful while you're asleep. Because of this, it's usually best not to put the rat cage in a bedroom or other sleeping area so the sound of rats at play won't wake you up throughout the night. It's also best to avoid putting the cage in a kitchen, for the sake of both rat and human health. Kitchens are more prone to shifts in the air temperature because of the heat put off by cooking, and if your rats manage to slip out of their enclosure, there are a whole host of troublesome things they could get into, from cleaning products in cabinets to the hot coils in the back of the fridge. It's also best to avoid putting rats in any food preparation areas because of the risk of cross-contamination, should your rats be carrying any illnesses. Rats will enjoy being around their people regularly, but may get stressed out by an environment that's extremely chaotic. A room with excessive noise, vibrations, or activity is not the best for your rat cage. Areas that get moderate activity are best, like a family room, home office, or living room.

Bedding and litter options

There's a subtle difference between the terms

bedding and litter when we're talking about small

rodent cages. Litter is for collecting the rats' waste to

keep it from pooling or accumulating on the cage

floor. The main characteristic you're looking for is

something absorbent that won't promote bacterial

growth. Bedding, on the other hand, should also be

soft enough for the rats to use as nesting material. Some materials are only suitable as litter, some only as bedding, and some are both soft and absorbent enough to be used as either. If you're using an under-cage litter tray or in-cage litter box, you should use a different material for litter than you do for bedding. This will help to differentiate the areas of the cage for both you and your rats.

Don't use clumping or clay kitty litters in rat enclosures. The dust from these products can irritate the lungs and skin. They also have a tendency to stick to paws, tails, and belly fur when the rat walks through, leading to a messy enclosure. Beddings made of corncob also aren't recommended. While it's good for bedding to be absorbent, corncobs are a little too absorbent. This leads to mold and bacteria build-up, and may reduce the humidity in the enclosure too much, leading to ailments like ringtail. Corncob beddings especially shouldn't be used with nursing mothers and weanlings.

Wood shavings

Wood shavings can be used as either bedding or litter for your rats, and are an excellent option for a glass aquarium or tank without a litter pan—if you choose the right kind of wood. Hardwoods, like aspen, are the only recommended wood shavings. Never use beddings made of cedar or pine. These were once popular for housing rats because of how well they eliminate odors. Unfortunately, the same compounds in these woods that make them smell so good--oils known as phenols—are also harmful to small animals. They can irritate the respiratory tract, cause problems with the skin, and build up in the blood, leading to kidney and liver problems. You should also avoid using soft woods as shavings in general. Because they're so absorbent, softer woods have a greater tendency to sprout bacteria and mold than harder woods.

Aspen wood shavings are absorbent and good at controlling odor. They're also biodegradable and flushable in small quantities. If you use wood shavings, you may also want to provide your rats with some scraps of cloth or shredded paper to use as nesting material. The main disadvantage of wood shavings is that they tend to be a little dustier than paper options.

Recycled paper beddings

Like wood shavings, recycled paper products can be used as either litter or bedding, and are great for glass aquaria and wire cages alike. Recycled paper is dust-free and soft enough to use in nesting. It's also highly absorbent, though it may not be as good at controlling odor as wood shaving beddings. Recycled paper is also easy to spot clean, and is light enough in color to allow you to see where it's been soiled and keep an eye on changes in your rat's droppings or urine.

The main disadvantage of recycled paper beddings is the cost, typically $20-$30 per bag, which can add up especially if you have lots of rats and a large enclosure. If you have more time than money, you can make your own recycled paper bedding out of junk mail or scrap paper. Just make sure to take out any glossy pieces or non-paper items (plastic windows from envelopes, staples, etc.) then rip the paper up and put it in a bowl in the sink. Soak the paper in the water, pulling it apart with your fingers. When the water gets too gray to see your hands, drain it and refill it, and continue pulling the paper apart. Repeat this process until the water in the bowl stays relatively clear, then mound the paper up into balls and allow it to dry. When you pull it apart, it will look very similar to the recycled paper beddings you find in the store. This can be an especially fun activity to do with kids.

Pelleted litters

You can find pelleted litters in the small animal section made of a wide variety of materials: Paper, wood pulp, and alfalfa or hay are the most common. These are great products for a litter pan or tray, though they're not soft enough to use as a rat's bedding and shouldn't be used as the primary litter in a glass aquarium, though they could work in a litter tray inside the aquarium.

Pelleted litters are very absorbent and generally good at controlling odors. They can be spot-cleaned daily with a litter scoop or designated slotted spoon, but should be changed fully once a week to prevent the build-up of ammonia and bacteria. Those made from organic materials—like hay and alfalfa—are also biodegradable and compostable, breaking down easily when wet.

Cloth cage liners

Sold online and in the small animal section of the pet store, cloth cage liners can be especially useful in multi-level enclosures at keeping the cage clean. Fleece is an excellent material for this because it's hydrophobic, meaning it's capable of absorbing less than 1% of its weight in water. This prevents the formation of wet spots where bacteria can grow. Cloth liners work well as the flooring in a metal cage. You can use a pelleted litter or pieces of paper towel or newsprint in the tray beneath to absorb liquids that leak through. Since they're washable and re-usable, cloth cage liners are cheaper in the long run than disposable bedding options. How frequently you need to change the liner will depend on how many rats you have in the enclosure, but you should keep enough on hand to change them 2-4 times a week and still have time to wash them—most keepers find it helpful to keep between 3 and 8 sets on-hand. You'll also need to use some kind of supplementary nesting material if you're using cloth liners. Shredded paper, recycled paper bedding, and scraps of cloth are all good options.

Cage furnishings

At the minimum, you'll need to have food and water containers, a hide box or sleeping area, and wood to chew on. You should also give your rats a wheel, climbing ropes, or some other kind of toy to keep them entertained and give them a chance to exercise. Rats can be litter boxed trained. They're relatively neat animals in general, and will likely use one corner of their cage most often for a bathroom even if not provided with a litter box, but having one can make it easier to clean the enclosure.

With all cage furnishings, the main things that should concern you are safety, durability, and ease of cleaning. Items made of porous materials—like wood blocks supplied to chew on, or cardboard tubes as tunnels—should be checked daily and removed once they've been soiled. Items made of metal should contain no zinc, because of the aforementioned potential reaction with the rat's urine. You should assume that anything put inside the rat's enclosure will be chewed on, so items that don't come from a pet store should be washed before going into the rat's cage, and you should make sure anything you give them uses non-toxic paints and materials. Finally, be mindful of anything that could catch a rat's toes or tail and cause injury. Take care with fabrics like terrycloth that have loops or fraying threads that can catch toes.

Food dishes

If there's anything in your enclosure your rats are guaranteed to chew on, it's their food dishes. You want to find a product that will be easy to clean and stand up to the constant jumping, climbing, and running your pets will subject it to. Because the dish will probably get trampled during nightly play sessions, you should also find a product that won't be easily tipped over. If you have a wire cage, you can often find durable food dishes that can be mounted to the bars to prevent spilling. If you have a glass or acrylic aquarium, you'll want to look instead for something that's low, wide, and bottom heavy. The ceramic or earthenware dishes you can find in the small animal section will work better than stand-alone stainless steel dishes, which are lightweight and will quickly become toys for inquisitive rats if they're not bolted down.

In terms of material, you should avoid anything made of plastic or wood. Your rats will chew both of these materials to shreds in no time. Wood has the extra disadvantage of being very absorbent, making it hard to clean. As mentioned above, ceramic and stainless steel are great options. Thick glass can also work, just remember that your rats will be standing on their dishes, and you shouldn't use anything that will crack or chip under the strain. Regardless of which material you go with, it's a good idea to keep two on hand so you can rotate them out, cleaning one when the other's in the cage.

Water bottles

It's better to use water bottles than water dishes with rats. Just like with their food bowls, rats will run through, poop in, and knock over a water dish, leaving them with nothing to drink and you with a good-sized mess to clean up. Bottles of either glass or plastic are fine—plastic bottles are easier to find at the local pet shop, while glass bottles are more durable in the long-term. Just like with food dishes, it's a good idea to get two so you can rotate them, giving you time to clean the bottle without your rats getting thirsty.

Nesting and hiding boxes

Female rats, especially, will often make their own nests out of the bedding you provide, but you should still give them somewhere they can hide. In the wild, rats will keep multiple nests throughout their territory, stocked with choice morsels of food and warm things to snuggle up in, just in case they get stranded far from home. Providing 1-2 hiding spots per rat is a good way to replicate this behavior inside your enclosure and give your pets a more natural environment.

If you're looking for hiding and sleeping spots in the small animal section of your pet store, you want to look at the sizes marketed for ferrets and guinea pigs—things designed for mice, gerbils, and hamsters will be too small to be comfortable. Suspended hammocks and snuggle bags made for ferrets and sugar gliders can make great sleeping or hiding spots for rats, and since they hang from the cage's walls or ceilings they're great space savers. Wooden nesting boxes work well, too, though you may need to replace these fairly often as your pets chew and pee on them. Depending on your rats, plastic igloo-style hideouts may work with some rats, though you should keep a careful eye on the item the first few days after you add it to the environment, and remove it if you notice a lot of bite marks.

Your rat's hide box doesn't have to come from a pet store. A length of PVC pipe can make a nice dark place for a rat to rest and relax. A ceramic flower pot turned on its side could be a cozy nest for a rat. Cleaned Pringles cans and cardboard boxes are nice temporary hide-outs, though you'll need to replace them every week or two. Provided the items you give them are non-toxic and large enough for them to get in and out of, your rats won't be picky.

Litter tray

Even if your cage came with a removable litter pan underneath, you may want to provide your rats with a litter box to help localize the waste. As with the hide boxes, you can use either items from the small animal section of the pet store or things you have around your home. Triangular ferret litter boxes fit nicely in a cage corner and are a good size for rats. You can also use low trays, like those designed for organizing drawers. The pan should be easy for the rats to climb in and out of and deep enough to contain the litter. It is worth nothing that while most rats will use their litter tray most of the time, there's no such thing as a housebroken rat. You should still check the bedding in the rest of the cage daily for waste, especially the areas around the food dishes and exercise wheel.

Exercise wheels

Female rats are generally more likely to use exercise wheels than males, but for either gender they can be a good way to provide your animals a chance to exercise between out of cage play sessions. When you're shopping for wheels, there are a few things you want to avoid. First, don't get a wheel whose running track is made of metal bars. These gaps are just wide enough for a rat's tail or leg to slip through and get caught and can lead to fractured limbs and other injuries. You should also pay close attention to the support structure for the wheel. Avoid anything with a central axle, which can catch a rat's tail. You should also avoid any support structures on the entry side of the wheel. Triangular supports can trap rats if they decide to step off their wheel mid-run, or catch a wayward tail.

Solid-track wheels like Wodent Wheels and Silent Spinners work well for rats. Get a model that's at least 12" in diameter—anything smaller will be too cramped. These designs are relatively quiet, as exercise wheels go, and you can buy track inserts that will help keep your rats' nails trimmed as they run (an added bonus). The disadvantage of these wheels is that they can be difficult to keep clean. Rats are likely to go to the bathroom while they're running, or to carry food and bedding onto the track. With the Wodent Wheel, the front cover must be completely removed before the track can be cleaned, which can be a hassle. Avoid the solid metal wheels designed for chinchillas—these are often too heavy for most rats to move, and they won't be likely to use them often.

Though you're not likely to find them in your local pet store, Stealth Wheels or Velociraptor Wheels are excellent for pet rats. These models have the same basic design. The running track is of ¼" poly coated wire, spaced to allow waste to fall through without injuring the rat who's running. They spin using a back-mounted ball bearing design that's one of the quietest on the market and also extremely durable. Like Wodent Wheels, these can come with a nail trimming insert, but the mostly-open front makes them easier to clean. Stealth Wheels can be found easily online through small animal breeders and suppliers.

If you have more horizontal than vertical space available, Flying Saucer wheel designs can also be used with rats. These wheels take the idea of the exercise wheel and turn it on its side, with a broad tilted plate that the rat can turn by running. It sometimes takes a little while for pets to figure out how to use these models—older male rats, especially, may never take to them—but they are safe and easy to clean. One complaint about Flying Saucer wheels is that they fling any food or waste on the wheel around the cage if the animal running builds up enough speed, so while the wheel itself is easy to clean, it may necessitate more cleaning of the space around it.

Other toys

While most toys in the small animal section will work for a rat, there are a couple of things you should avoid. Run-around balls or hamster balls should not be used with rats. These are the clear plastic balls that the pet sits inside, meant to let them run around without getting into trouble. These are dangerous for rats. A rat can only sweat through the pads of its feet, and the poor ventilation of hamster balls means they present an overheating risk. Also, while rats are big fans of climbing through mazes and tunnels, the ones you'll find designed for hamsters and gerbils will probably be too small. Look for the wider designs made for guinea pigs or ferrets.

Favorite toys of rats are things they can chew on and things they can climb on. Because a rat's teeth grow continuously throughout its life, you should always provide some kind of wooden object. The small animal section of the pet store is the obvious place to look for these, but you can also check the bird section—hanging wood toys available for birds satisfy both the chewing and climbing requirements and are sure to be beloved by your rats. Use caution with wooden toys for children—these may be suitable, but only if you're sure the wood hasn't been chemically pressed or treated.

In terms of cage furnishings, hanging toys for climbing help to maximize the space usage and keep your rats from getting bored. Lava Ledges in the small animal section are platforms for jumping and climbing that wear down your rat's toenails naturally and can be a great multi-purpose cage furnishing. In the small animal section, you can also get cloth swings and tunnels made for ferrets. The bird section is a great place to find ladders and climbing ropes.

You also don't have to limit yourself to the pet store. PVC pipes from the hardware store can be used to set up mazes, either inside the cage or during outside playtime. Children's toys are also great for rats, who will enjoy pushing balls around their cage, or looking for treats inside toy construction equipment. Because they're so active and intelligent, your rats can have a good time playing with almost anything, so use your imagination, swapping the toys around a couple times a month to keep the environment engaging.

Other supplies

It's a good idea to keep a kitchen scale on hand to help keep track of your rat's weight. Changes in food and water consumption are good early signs of a problem, but since rats rarely live alone and eat mostly at night, it can be difficult to tell who's eating what. Rats stop growing at around 9 months of age; their weight should increase gradually up to this point and then stay relatively constant. You should get a scale that takes measurements in increments of at least 2 grams, to get a truly accurate record.

If your rat isn't provided with ways to wear his nails down naturally, you'll probably need to trim them occasionally. A pair of cat claw trimmers will work well for this. There is a vein inside the nail, called the quick, which will bleed if nicked. You'll want to keep something on hand to stop the bleeding in case this happens. You can buy powders designed for this purpose, or just keep a small stash of flour or cornstarch with the clippers in case this happens. If you don't feel comfortable trimming the nails yourself,

a local veterinarian should be able to assist.

Chapter 3: Care and Feeding

A rat's care is generally less involved than that of a cat or a dog. A rat that's handled daily will be better bonded to his humans and live a generally happier life, but rats that have cage-mates are also capable of being fairly self-sufficient, and probably won't hold it against you if you're too busy for daily playtime every once in a while. The main things you need to do every day are provide fresh food and water and keep the cage clean.

Bringing your rats home

The move to your home is a stressful for your pet rats. Your home is full of a wide array of different smells—at least to the rat's high developed nose. Give your rats some time to settle in before you start the bonding process. For the first 1-2 days, you should give your rats food and water and check on them occasionally, but otherwise don't handle them. They'll want to check out their boundaries and mark their territory in those first couple days, making it feel and smell like home.

If you already have a colony rats and are bringing home new animals to add to it, you want to quarantine them in a separate cage for 2-4 weeks before introducing them to the rest of your pets. The main reason for this is to prevent your new pets from spreading illnesses to the rest of your colony. Because moving puts stress on the rat's system, their immune system is lessened, and they are more likely to develop health problems during the first couple weeks of ownership than they otherwise would be. This is especially true of pet store rats, who are kept in larger colonies and exposed to more potential viruses, parasites, and bacteria. New rats in quarantine should be kept as far as possible from the established colony (it's best to put them in a separate room). When it comes time for cleaning and play, interact with your established colony first, so your hands and clothes don't carry any ailments from one cage to the other.

Regardless of whether these are your first rats or if you're adding them to an existing colony, there's a few extra things you can do to start them off right. It's always a good idea to take your new pets to a vet shortly after bringing them home. A lot of ailments that affect rats can be reversed or cured if they're caught early. A reputable breeder will have raised the rats in such a way as to prevent most chronic issues, but rats from a pet store aren't likely to have received the same care and attention, and it's especially important to take these animals for an initial check-up to avoid problems down the road.

Rats are naturally shy, and a lot of light, movement, and sound can make them anxious. Rats that live with people eventually get used to their voices and daily rhythms, but in the first couple weeks try to keep them out of the limelight as much as possible. If the cage's permanent home will be a center of household activity, like a living room, keep them in a quieter space instead for their first couple weeks. If that's not possible, you can partially cover the cage with a blanket or towel—just make sure to leave at least one side clear to provide ample ventilation and to check on your rats to make sure they're not overheating.

Bonding with your new rats

Even though animals like humans, dogs, and cats would be a rat's enemies in the wild, domestic rats can form close and affectionate bonds with these natural adversaries, provided you establish a solid foundation of trust early in the animal's life. Patience is your most important tool in bonding with your rats. Stay calm in all your interactions with the animal while you're bonding—rats are able to pick up on tension in humans, and will react in kind by getting skittish and defensive. The amount of time it takes a rat to trust you will depend mostly on the personality on the animal. Some will be inquisitive and want to explore you right away; others may take a week or more to approach you. Don't get discouraged if it seems to be taking your animal a while to adjust, especially if you got it from a pet store or rescue organization. You can win over even the shyest rat with enough time and patience.

After your new rat's 1-2 day settling in period, you can put your hand into the cage for your new rats to sniff. Move slowly when you do this. Rats have very bad eyesight and are easily startled by sudden movements. If your rats run away instead of sniffing your hand, try offering them a tasty treat—a bit of fruit, a dog biscuit, or a treat like yogurt drops from the small animal section. The smell of the food will prompt the rats to investigate, and eventually they'll start to associate your smell with getting treats and seek you out when you're around.

Extroverted rats—especially the females—will often start to explore their new humans with little prompting after a couple days of sniffing. If your rat doesn't take this first step, slowly and gently slide your hands underneath him to pick him up, then sit with him in an enclosed, neutral space. A bed or couch can be good for this—somewhere that the rat can retreat, but not so far it's hard to find him. Keep lots of treats on hand and reward the rat for positive behavior. Give him a treat if he sits calmly and lets you stroke him, for example, or the first few times he comes to your hand willingly. Again, your goal here is to build positive associations with your smell.

Though a colony of rats can be self-sufficient once it's established, in the first month or two with a new rat you should make it a point to spend at least 30 minutes of quality time with your pets every day. This can be hand-feeding them a meal, playing with them using mazes and toys, or simply letting them cuddle in your lap while you're watching TV. Play off of your animal's natural instincts. If he seems to want quiet time, don't force him to be active—and vice versa. Food is pretty much always a winner. Of course, if you have more than 30 minutes to spend with your rats, go for it. The more time you spend together, the more bonding will happen.

Generally speaking, the younger the rat, the easier time you'll have forming a bond with it. Which is not to say adult rats can't become great pets—simply that you may need to take a little bit longer to get them used to you. With any age of animal, you should never use physical force in training or disciplining the animals. Not only is it cruel, it's also ineffective. A rat's brain doesn't work the same way as a human's. If you strike it or yell at it, it won't associate that with its actions, but with you, the person who's yelling at it. This will ultimately only serve to make the rat less receptive to you and less trusting of you in the future. Positive reinforcement of good behavior works much better for rats in the long run.

Introducing new rats to a colony

Age and gender are going to be the main factors in how easily your pet rats take to new cagemates. The instinct to recognize dominance hierarchies develops around 10 weeks of age, so it's easiest to introduce new rats to each other before this age. Adult females generally take a bit longer to welcome newcomers into the cage, and adult males are the hardest to introduce to each other. If you're buying a companion for an older animal whose cagemate died, consider buying a pair of younger rats together. Three rats don't need significantly more space than two, and these two younger rats will keep each other company while the older rat's figuring out whether or not she likes them. This will also prevent you from having to repeat the introduction process for your new pet when the older rat dies.

After the 2-4 week quarantine, move the two cages as close to each other as possible so the rats can get accustomed to each other's scents. Swapping cage items can be helpful to speed the process along. If you use any cloth cage furnishings, like hammocks or snuggle bags, those will be most likely to hold scents and will be great things to swap. Alternatively, a small amount of nesting material could do the trick. Let them hang out side by side for about a week before attempting face-to-face introductions.

You should introduce your animals on neutral territory, outside of either cage. Like with your initial bonding with the animal, a bed or couch works well for this. If you're introducing animals into a large colony, the alpha's approval is what he'll need to gain acceptance. Every colony of rats will have an alpha animal, even if they're exclusively female; you'll know which animal is the alpha because he or she will be the first one to the food dish and will be the winner of any in-cage squabbles. If you have a larger established colony and don't want to have to worry about keeping track of all of them during the first few introductions, introduce your new pets to the alpha separately from the rest of the group. Since the other animals are accustomed to being subservient, they will be less likely to squabble with your new rats. Separating that dominant animal out lets you pay better individual attention during the more sensitive introduction.

If your new rats fight when you put them on neutral turf, separate the animals back into their respective cages and try again the next day. You can often make them stop fighting by gently spraying both animals with clean water in a plant mister. The rats will stop fighting to groom themselves. If they still fight after a couple attempts, there's a few things you can try. A dab of vanilla extract on the nose, genitals, and chest of all animals being introduced should level the playing field slightly, encouraging them to circle, sniff, and lick each other. If your rats are female, you could wait until the alpha is in heat and then try the introductions. Mock mating can be a great bonding activity to bring these new rats into the fold, and your alpha doe will at least be a bit distracted and less likely to respond to perceived intruders on her turf. If you disinfect the alpha's cage, it should lessen the territorial instincts, and may make him or her more receptive to the newbies. Alternatively, putting items in the introduction area that carry the new animal's scent—like furnishings, bedding, or the litter pan from her cage—could shift the balance of power long enough for some bonding to happen.

Once your rats all seem to be getting along during play time, you can safely put the new animals in with the established colony. It's a good idea to disinfect the cage and its furnishings first—again, the less the alpha smells him or herself in the enclosure, the less territorial the animal will be. Pay extra close attention to the cage for the first few days after the introduction, and keep your secondary cage ready to go, just in case the animals start fighting.

Younger rats (less than a year old) should accept each other within a couple weeks of first being introduced. With older rats, the process could take up to a month, especially if one or both of them have always lived alone. Very rarely, certain rats simply won't get along with each other. You should be prepared to continue housing them separately, on the off chance this should happen.

Food and nutrition

Rats should be given fresh food and water every day. They prefer to eat at night, so the best time to give your rats their daily meal is early evening—right around dinner time for humans. A single adult rat's per day consumption is about 5 grams of food for every 100 grams of body weight, meaning about 25 grams for the average adult male and about 15 grams for the average adult female. The rat's lifestyle and metabolism also have an effect on how much food they should eat per day. Up to about the age of 9 months, rats are still growing rapidly and should be given about twice that much. Keep a close eye on how much food your rats are eating. If there's a little bit left over at the end of the night that's fine, but if they're consistently refusing food that could be a sign of illness. Rats do tend to hoard choice morsels of food in their nests, so check the bedding first to make sure they're not just eating from a private stash.

Because they've been used so extensively for medical research, a lot more is known about their nutritional needs than with most other pets, and it's relatively easy to find commercial rat food that satisfies its full nutritional needs. If you're using a commercial food, it's a good idea to supplement it with fresh fruits and vegetables to maintain dietary variety—about 80% commercial food and 20% fresh.

About 7-15% of an adult rat's diet should be protein. This does not necessarily need to be animal protein; nuts and seeds also provide good protein. Babies younger than 4 months and pregnant or nursing mothers should have their protein increased, to about 15-20% of their diet, to aid in either growth or recovery. The main nutrients of concern for rats are A, E, and the B vitamins. Commercial rat chows are specifically formulated to provide these nutrients in the right ratios, and if you're using a commercial chow you shouldn't give your rat vitamin or mineral supplements unless specifically instructed to do so by your vet. Doing so runs the risk of over supplementing, especially when it comes to fat-soluble vitamins that can accumulate in the system and cause kidney or liver damage.

Rats are opportunistic feeders and can eat almost anything you can eat, with a few notable exceptions. You should never give your rats licorice, rhubarb, poppy, or bitter almonds, which have a higher cyanide content than their sweet cousins. Rats are sensitive to fungi and mold, and blue cheese could be toxic to rats. Raw peanuts contain antinutrients that can destroy enzymes in the rats system it needs to digest and shouldn't be fed to rats. Roasted peanuts are fine, though their high fat content means they should only be used as treats. Male rats may develop kidney problems from ingesting certain tropical and citrus fruits, so avoid mangoes, oranges, grapefruits, and lemons when feeding your bucks (though they're fine for does).

The myth that a small amount of a carbonated beverage (soda pop or beer) can kill your rat is false, but you still shouldn't give them any drinks with lots of chemicals, especially anything containing caffeine or alcohol. Fruit juice is better for an occasional sugary treat. Though rats love nuts, you shouldn't give them any kind of nut butter because of its texture—it's so sticky it jams up a rat's jaws, sometimes even suffocating him. This goes for other sticky foods, as well.

Generally speaking, even when you're giving your rats treats you should limit the amount of fat they get in their diet to lessen the risk of obesity. Their diet should be heavier on grains and vegetables than it is on seeds, nuts, and meats, and anything a human would consider "junk food" should be given to them very sparingly. So while chocolate isn't toxic to rats the same way it is to dogs, you still shouldn't let your little guys have very much of it.

Some keepers like to feed their rats exclusively on fresh foods, and there's certainly nothing wrong with that if you have the time to prepare your rats a complete nutritionally balanced meal every day. For most people, though, pelleted chows and mixes are a more convenient—and equally suitable—way to give your rats a balanced diet.

Lab blocks

As their name would suggest, lab blocks were formulated to provide a complete nutritional diet to rats being kept for studies without introducing any variables that could sway the results. These brown or greyish blocks may not look very appetizing, but they've been specifically designed to keep captive rats at optimal health. Popular brands of lab blocks for pet rats are Harlan Teklad, Oxbow, Kaytee, and Mazuri. Make sure you're buying the appropriate formula for your rat's age—those made for young and growing rats have more protein than those designed for adults.

Your local pet store might or might not carry lab blocks in their small animal section. If they don't, you can find them easily online for around $10-15 for a 5 pound bag. The advantage of these products over small animal grain mixes is that each mouthful of a lab block is nutritionally complete, and doesn't leave the rat the option of picking out his favorite bits.

Small animal grain mixes

There is a lot of variety on the shelf when it comes to mixes for small animals, and their labeling can be both misleading and confusing. Not every food that says it's for rats will actually be formulated correctly for their needs, while some packaged for other rodents could work perfectly well. Regardless of what animal's picture is on the label, you should check the ingredients of any packaged grain mix before you buy it. Avoid any mix that contains dried corn. Corn is fine for rats in small quantities but it has high nitrate levels and cause stomach cancers if rats eat too much.

Improperly stored corn is also prone to growing certain molds that are very bad for a rat's digestive system. Rats aren't big fans of alfalfa pellets and will probably not eat them, so you shouldn't buy a mix that's alfalfa-pellet based or you'll end up throwing away a lot of food. The mix should have a protein content of around 12-14%, with a fat content no more than 5%. Soybean meal is a good ingredient to look for when you're feeding female rats, as soy products have been shown to decrease the growth of mammary tumors.

The advantage of grain mixes is that they more closely mimic the natural feeding habits of wild rats, and gives them more dietary variety, which can keep them from getting bored with their food. The disadvantage, as mentioned above, is that they may pick out the pieces they like, either eating it and leaving the rest or hiding it around the cage where it could grow bacteria and spoil. You could strike a balance by using grain mixes a few days a week and lab blocks on the other days, giving them dietary variety while still making sure they're eating a nutritious and complete diet.

Fresh diets

There's a thriving online community of rat breeders and fanciers, many of whom have published their own versions of a complete home-made rat diet on their blogs and websites for your perusal. The challenge with creating a rat diet from scratch is that no single product is going to be able to provide them with all the vitamins and minerals they need. Just like with commercial mixes, you're looking to achieve around 10% protein content for adult rats (15-20% for young rats and breeding females), with a fat content of 5% or less. Rats can produce some vitamins they need within their own bodies, but you need to make sure you're giving them sufficient amounts of B, A, and E vitamins. An easy rule of thumb for feeding adult rats is to consider an amount of food that's the size of their head to be one serving. Every day, each rat should be given about 1 serving of grains, 2 servings of vegetables, and half a serving of fruit.

For the grains, you can use dry rolled oats, unsalted soy nuts, dry pasta, high protein flake cereals (like Total or Special K) or lightly sweetened puffed wheat cereal (plain Cheerios, Quaker, several Kashi varieties). Combine any three or more from the above list to give the mix more nutritional variety.

For the vegetables, you again want to give your rats a wide variety to choose from, to make sure they're getting all their nutrients. Sweet potatoes, cooked beans, broccoli, kale, collard greens, and bok choy are great for rats, and half your daily vegetable offerings should be made up of one or more of the above. Supplement this with a smattering of other veggies and herbs, like tomato, parsley, squash, peas, and carrots.

Fruits are going to give your rats a lot of great vitamins, and again, variety is key. Rats love berries, apples, and melons, and will also happily eat plums, grapes, raisins, and bananas. Like mentioned above, avoid citrus fruits and mangoes with male rats, but you can include these in the diets of female rats without issues.

Rats will also need to be given a serving of protein 3-4 days a week. This can be made up of nuts and seeds if you want to keep your rat vegetarian, but rats are omnivores and will enjoy a bit of animal protein in their diet. Any meats you feed your rats should be cooked, free of preservatives or seasonings, and relatively lean—turkey and chicken are better than beef or pork. Rats can also be given protein from less traditional sources. Cooked beef liver or canned oysters can be a great way to get rats some of the more esoteric minerals, like copper, that could be lacking in the rest of their diet.

If you're doing a home-made recipe, it's recommended to research the rat's nutritional needs thoroughly, either through online forums or by asking your veterinarian. Though fresher food is arguably more similar to a rat's diet in the wild, lab blocks have

the distinct advantage of having figured out the rat's

nutrition for you, leaving you less of a chance to miss

something and cause a nutritional deficiency that

could impact your rat's health long-term.

Treats

Just like people, rats love to eat foods that aren't

very good for them. They have an especially strong

taste for things that are sweet, fatty, or both. Scraps

from your meals can make good occasional treats, as

long as you check what you're eating against the list

of dangerous foods for rats.

Many pre-packaged treats sold in the small animal

section are just the same ingredients used in pelleted

food, but with some kind of sweetener added to make

them taste better. Your rats will probably enjoy these

products, but they're essentially just more expensive

versions of lab blocks. If you're looking for pre-packaged treats, yogurt drops are often a better option. They also enjoy dog biscuits and certain cat treats, though again, you should give these items only in moderation due to the high fat content.

Proper food storage

When you're using fresh food, it's very obvious when the food has gone bad. With lab blocks or prepackaged mixes, it can be harder to tell that you're feeding your pet spoiled foods. The nutrients in these foods breaks down over time, while the nuts and seeds in grain mixes can spoil and go rancid, making them potentially harmful or, at the least, unappetizing. Always check the expiration dates on any products you're buying in the pet store, and don't buy a larger bag than you're likely to use in a month. The food will spoil more quickly once the bag is open.

Heat and moisture can make food break down faster, so always keep your rat's food in an air-tight container in a cool, dry place. Check it often for any signs of mold. Nuts and seeds put off a rancid odor when they start to spoil, so if you smell anything off in the bag, it's probably best to throw it away.

Water

Rats should have fresh water available to them at all times. When you give your rats their daily meal, you should also remove the water bottle, either switching it out for a spare or emptying, washing, and refilling it before putting it back on the cage. A healthy adult rat drinks an average of 2 ounces of water per day. Keep a close eye on your rats' water consumption—changes can be a sign that they're developing an illness.

Vitamin C supplements for water sold in the small animal section of the pet store are designed for use with guinea pigs, not rats. Rats given a healthy diet will need no additional vitamin C in their diet, and adding supplements to their water can ultimately be harmful, promoting bacterial growth that could make your pets sick.

Playtime and handling

Daily play time is the best way to form a close bond with your rats. It's also good for your pets' health—even with a large enclosure and ample tools for exercise, your rats are active creatures and need time to run around outside their cage. Any space you let your rats out into will need to be rat-proofed for their safety, and you should supervise them carefully the entire time they're out of the cage.

You should make sure there are no living hazards in the space before you let your rats out. Dogs and cats are often bred specifically for their ability to catch rats and other rodents, and unless you have very well-trained and gentle animals, you're risking your rats' health by introducing them to these natural predators. The same thing is true of other pet species that are natural predators of rats, like snakes and certain carnivorous lizards.

So far as the space itself, remember that rats love to both chew and climb. Any surface that they can get a toe-hold on will be fair game for exploration, and they are capable of squeezing into very tight spaces, meaning you have to be careful all harmful materials are either removed from the space or stored securely in locking cabinets. Make sure there's no appliances they could climb into or any electrical cords they could chew on, and that any radiators or heating vents are blocked off.

Some rats enjoy swimming, and provided you supervise them carefully and give them dry areas they can climb out onto when they're ready, you could have fun turning your bathtub into a rat swimming pool. Make sure the water is lukewarm and that you have a towel on hand to dry them off when they get out so they don't get too cold. It should be noted that while most rats are good swimmers, not all will enjoy it. If your rat doesn't seem to want to play in the water, don't force the issue. There are plenty of other ways for your rats to get playtime and exercise.

Correctly handling your rat

You should never pick up a rat from above or by the tail. This is the way a lot of predators would grab a rat, and it will trigger an instinctual fear reaction from your animal. Once you're bonded with the animal, your best option will probably be to simply put your hand in the cage and call the rat's name, and it will often come to you eagerly. If you do need to physically pick up your pet, slide your hand underneath it slowly and gently lift up so the animal feels secure and doesn't try to escape.

A rat's first instinct when it's feeling defensive is to flee, not to bite, but it will use its teeth as a last resort if it feels cornered or trap. Never grab a rat so tightly it feels like it can't get away. This is especially important advice for the parents of young children, who often want to grab a rat harder than the animal wants to be held. Stress the importance of gentle handling with your children, and wait until you've bonded successfully with the animals to introduce them to younger kids. A good way to start is to have the child sit on a couch with their palms cupped in their lap and set the rat into their palms. Tell them to let it explore them without trying to handle it first. Once it knows their scent, they can try some gentle petting, eventually graduating to picking up the rat themselves once they've learned how much pressure is okay to use.

Cleaning and grooming schedules

Rats are naturally fairly clean animals, but you should still set up a daily, weekly, and monthly cleaning and care schedule to prevent ammonia and bacteria from building up in their environment. Soapy water is fine for regular cleaning of ceramic, plastic, or metal cage furnishings. Cloth items can be machine washed with an unscented detergent. Wood furnishings can be wiped off with a damp cloth, and should be checked often for mold growth; if you see any, dispose of the item. Cardboard items should be disposed of when they're soiled.

If an illness or parasite affects your rats, you should thoroughly disinfect the cage and all its furnishings. In this case, you should throw away any wood items, as well as the rat's nesting material and bedding, and any cardboard in the cage. All other items can be disinfected with a solution of 1 part bleach to 10 parts water. Rinse the items thoroughly after washing them until there's no scent of bleach remaining on the item. Cloth furnishings can be soaked in disinfectant and then machine washed until the bleach smell dissipates. Wipe down the inside of the cage with clean water after disinfecting it to make sure no bleach residue stays behind.

Daily care

Your daily care should start with removing any of the previous day's food from the enclosure. You should also remove and empty their bottle at this point, replacing its contents with fresh water. If your rats use a litter pan or tray, scoop out any soiled litter. If you're using recycled paper or wood shavings as a bedding, you should spot-clean them daily. If you're using cloth cage liners, you should check them daily and replace them no less frequently than twice per week. While you're at it, you should also check any other toys, climbing shelves, or hide boxes for messes to wipe up, and check all cloth cage furnishings for wet spots. Once all this is done, give your rats their new food and to let them out of their cage for play and exercise.

Some keepers find it easiest to do all of this checking and cleaning while the rats are out having their playtime. Others think it's easier to do it during the day, when they're not generally as active, or while they're distracted by their nightly meal. Since rats don't have a strict sleeping and waking schedule like some other animals, you aren't likely to disrupt your pets' natural rhythm by interacting with them during the daytime. Rats can easily adapt their schedule to yours, but whatever time of day you play with and feed your rats, it works best to do it at on a relatively consistent schedule whenever possible.

Weekly care

If you only have a pair of rats, you should only need to thoroughly replace the bedding and litter once a week. Larger colonies may need to have it changed twice a week. Regardless of how many rats you have, you should remove all the furnishings from inside the cage weekly. Clean solid objects with soapy water and machine wash any cloth items. Make sure to also clean out the inside of your water bottles using a bristled brush.

If you use a litter pan or box, scrub that thoroughly as well before refilling it with fresh litter and returning it to the cage. A lot of rat keepers will keep groups of toys and furnishings and switch them out when they do the weekly cage cleaning. This isn't necessarily something you have to do, but variety in the things your rats are presented to play with will help keep them from getting bored.

Monthly care

The most important thing you can do for your rats on a monthly basis is weigh them. It's a good idea to keep a ledger of some kind for this information so you can track any changes, keying you into potential issues with their health. You should also check your rats' toenails and teeth when you do this. Both teeth and nails grow continuously. If the nails are getting too long, you can trim them with a pair of cat claw trimmers. If the teeth are getting too long, or if they don't seem to be lining up inside your rat's mouth, you should call your vet.

About once a month, you should also give the inside of the cage a good scrub with soapy water. It's easiest to do this while the bedding, litter pan, and cage furnishings have been removed for cleaning. Make sure to dry it thoroughly before replacing the bedding to keep wet spots from forming. Cages with lots of rats (4 or more) may need to be scrubbed down two times a month.

Bathing your rats

Rats are fastidious self-groomers and don't need to be bathed too regularly—about two times a year should do it. You should take care not to bathe your rat too frequently, in fact, or you risk stripping too many of the natural oils from the fur, making their skin dry. The exception to this is if your rats are sick or elderly and have difficulty self-grooming, in which case you can give them a gentle sponge bath whenever their fur starts to look dirty or matted.

If your rats enjoy swimming for fun, you'll probably have no problem getting them in a couple inches of water to clean off. If your rats are less comfortable with water, you can give them a sponge bath instead. Only use lukewarm water when you're bathing your rats so they don't get overheated. Even if your rats swim around together at playtime, you should only bathe one at a time, to keep yourself from getting distracted.

Have a towel ready whenever you bathe your rat so you can dry him off right away and he doesn't get too chilly. Fill two smooth-sided containers with an inch or two of lukewarm water. If you're giving your rat a sponge bath, put a clean sponge in each of the buckets, and have a third container to keep your rat in while you're washing him. You could also give him a sponge bath in a stoppered sink or tub. Wet your rat's back and apply a few drops of cat shampoo, gently massaging it into a lather with your fingertips. Don't use a bristled brush—you could scrub too hard without realizing it and irritate your pet's skin. Be especially careful when you're cleaning around the face to not get any soap into the eyes, ears, or nose.

Once your rat's thoroughly scrubbed, it's time to rinse. Pick him up and move him to the second container. If you're giving a sponge bath, wring water from the clean sponge over the rat's back until most of the lather is gone, then use the sponge to get the rest. Don't try to rinse your rat under a faucet. The water pressure will be too high and will stress your rat out, even if it doesn't cause any direct injuries. The same goes for the spray attachment on your kitchen sink.

Nail trimming

Some rats may never need their nails trimmed, especially if they're given items around their cage to help wear them down. From the perspective of the animal's health, you only have to trim the nails if they start to grow back in toward the toe. A lot of times, a rat's nails are trimmed for the human's sake. Long rat nails can leave serious scratches when they climb on you. If this doesn't concern you, you may never have to worry about nail trimming. If you think these scratches will be an issue for you, you should start trimming as start as soon as possible (within the first couple months of bringing the animal home) so your pet can adjust to the process.

The hardest part about trimming a rat's nails is getting it to stay still. You can wrap your rat gently in a towel and extend one paw at a time if he absolutely refuses to stay put, but you'll find it much easier if you can get your rat to stop fighting you in the first place. Don't try to trim all of your rat's nails in one go on your first attempt. Do as many as you can before he starts to get fidgety, then give him a treat and let him relax. A couple days later, pick up where you left off, again stopping and giving the rat treats when he starts squirming. Provided you don't nick the quick, toe-trimming is completely painless for the rat, and the treats should help him get over the weirdness of the process, making him more and more comfortable and relaxed each time he does it.

There is a vein running down the center of a rat's nail (called the quick) that will hurt and bleed if it's cut. The quick looks like a pink streak in the center of the nail. You should only trim the part of the nail above this, where it's completely white. Cornstarch and flour both work well to help stop the bleeding if you do accidentally catch the quick, and you should keep a small plate nearby when you're trimming your rat's nails just in case.

Vacation and travel

Your rats should be fine in the house by themselves if you're just going away on an overnight trip, or even for the weekend, as long as you make sure to give them plenty of food and fresh water. If you're going away longer than that, the best option is to find a pet sitter who will come to your home. Kennels are very stressful environments for rats. Not only will they be assaulted by a whole new array of smells, kennels are typically not very calm or quiet environments, and the abundance of strange animals can be frightening. It's much better for their health to keep them in the comfort of their own home.

If you have to take your rat in the car—like to the vet, or a pet show—you should always transport him in some kind of container. This can be your substitute cage or a small pet carrier like those designed for cats. Even well-behaved rats can be a distraction while you're driving and it's safer for everybody if you keep the animal contained. If it's cold out, warm the car up before bringing your rat out and cover the carrier with a blanket to keep it from losing too much heat. If it's hot out, make sure your animals aren't in direct sunlight.

Chapter 4: Health and Breeding

The majority of common health issues that affect rats can be prevented through proper care and nutrition. Tumors are frequent issues with older rats, especially with unneutered females. The most common ailments affecting younger rats are respiratory infections and injuries sustained while climbing and jumping. The best way to prevent illness in your rats is to remove as many stressors as possible. Factors that cause stress in rats include cramped quarters, dirty enclosures, sudden temperature changes, spoiled food, and excessive noise or light. Keeping your rats well-fed and watered and their cage clean are imperative to long-term health and longevity. Weighing your rats regularly will also clue you in to developing health problems before they get serious.

Rats are highly adaptable and can recover from most ailments. Though they can be prone to more health problems as they age, this is often caused by the cumulative effects of a lifetime of improper nutrition or care. Aside from tumors and the occasional infection, a well-cared for rat should not require much medical treatment.

Finding a vet

It's not generally as difficult to find a vet to see your rats as it would be for more exotic small animals, like chinchillas or hedgehogs. If you live in a major metropolitan area, you'll probably have a few qualified vets to choose from. People in more rural areas may have to travel further. If you need help finding a vet, check out the Rat and Mouse Club of America's list of recommended vets.

Some people think that because rats are less expensive pets than cats or dogs they don't need to be taken to the vet for check-ups. The cost of an animal has nothing to do with its health, and while medical treatments for rats are typically cheaper than those for cats or dogs, you should still budget around $50 for a vet visit, and more if they require surgery or costly medications. It's a good idea to take your rat in for a health check at least once a year. This will help you to catch potentially expensive health problems earlier, and will give your vet a history with your rat, making it easier to treat him if a major problem should arise.

Signs of a problem

Rats are very stoic animals, not likely to show you when something's wrong. This is a defense mechanism in the wild, where sick and injured animals are the first targets of predators, but can make it difficult for you as a pet keeper to identify issues with your rats' health. The best way to tell if something is wrong with your pet rat is to know his usual behaviors and make note of any variations. Changes in eating and drinking habits, especially, can be a good early indicator of potential problems. If your rat's appetite seems to go away for longer than a day or two, you should call your vet. You should also keep an eye on your rats' droppings as you're cleaning the cage. They should be solid, hard, and dark in color. Moist or off-colored droppings are an indication of something awry in the digestive tract.

Rats are fastidious self-groomers, and issues with the coat can be a sign that something's wrong. A healthy rat's coat is uniform and sleek. Bald spots or a messy, ruffled, or puffy appearance to the fur could be a sign of skin problems. A thinning coat or scaly and flaky skin could mean some kind of infection or a vitamin deficiency. Reddish-brown discharge from the eyes and nose is a sign of environmental stress or an airborne irritant. This substance is called porphyrin, and though it sometimes looks like blood it's actually a lubricant for the eyelids. When irritated or infected, the rat's body will produce too much porphyrin, causing it to leak from the eyes and stain the face. While this isn't as serious as if you did see blood coming out of your rat's eyes (which would definitely be cause for alarm) you should still take note of the rat's environment when you see this and figure out what's causing the problem.

Rats that have poor balance or are holding their heads to one side may be suffering from an inner ear infection. This could also be a sign of a tumor or the result of a stroke in older rats, so you should take your animal to the vet just to be sure. Limping or favoring a paw is typically a sign of some kind of injury, and you should check on the animal, and take them to the vet if it doesn't get better within a couple of days.

Finally, wheezing, sneezing, labored breathing, discharge from the eyes and nose, lethargy, and diarrhea are signs your rat has some kind of infection, the severity of which can be difficult to determine. It may or may not require medical treatment, but if you notice any of these signs you should move the animal into quarantine to prevent the spread of infection to the other rats in your enclosure, and keep a close eye on them to see how the illness is progressing. If symptoms worsen, or if the rat refuses to eat or drink, you should call your vet immediately.

Spaying and neutering

It's your choice as a rat owner whether you want to spay or neuter your animals. If you're not planning on breeding your animals, spaying your female rats might be a good idea to prevent health issues down the line. Mammary tumors, urinary tract infections, certain cancers, and other reproductive issues are much rarer in spayed females. Spaying is an invasive procedure, and you and your vet should discuss the risks and benefits before you make the decision. It's generally a better idea for younger rats than older ones; female rats over 2 years of age are more likely to experience complications from the surgery.

Neutering males is most often done for behavioral reasons. Males that are very aggressive or are fighting a lot with their cage-mates will calm down after neutering. While this is still a surgical procedure, it's less invasive than spaying a female and carries fewer risks. Again, it's best done when the male is younger (around 9 months to a year). If you want to co-habitate males with females, it's better to neuter the males than to spay the females. Both procedures typically cost in the rage of $65 to $150, depending on your vet.

Respiratory infections

Issues with the upper respiratory tract are the most common in rats. Signs are similar to symptoms of the common cold in humans—sneezing, nasal discharge, and noisy breathing. You may also notice porphyrin stains around the eyes. Thoroughly disinfect the cage in addition to quarantining the sick animal. Quick action may prevent it from spreading to the rest of the colony.

One infection worth noting in particular is mycoplasma pulmonis. All rats in the domestic population carry this bacteria. It is what's known as an "opportunistic commensal," meaning it remains dormant in your rats, causing no problems, until something else weakens their immune system and leads to an active infection. If your rat does get a mycoplasma infection, it can be controlled with antibiotics but will never completely go away. Because of this, you can't simply let the illness "run its course"—a rat affected by mycoplasma should get veterinary treatment to keep the problem from worsening.

Respiratory infections left untreated for too long may develop into pneumonia, especially in older rats. Pneumonia causes progressive damage to the animal's lungs. They'll have difficulty breathing and may refuse food or water, eventually leading to death.

Skin problems

Skin problems in rats can be caused either by environmental factors or by an infection. If you notice a lot of scabs on your rat's face and shoulders, this could be due to too much protein in your animal's diet. This can cause itchy spots on your rat's skin, prompting them to scratch and hurt themselves. Reduce high-protein offerings like peanuts, sunflower seeds, or any meats, and see if the issue resolves itself. If it doesn't, this could be a sign of mites. Mites are microscopic creatures, about the size of a pin-head, that infest the fur and skin of many animal species. You can tell if your rat has mites by rubbing his fur with your hand over a towel. You'll likely dislodge some of the mites and see them moving around on the cloth. Most mite infestations don't require veterinary treatment. Thoroughly disinfect the cage, replace the bedding and any wood furnishings, and then bathe your rats in a cat-safe flea and tick shampoo. Dust the new bedding lightly with a cat flea powder for 1-2 weeks. If the mites persist, then you should call your vet to seek further treatment.

Mange is an advanced mite infection, most often found in conjunction with other issues. When an animal's immune system is compromised from an illness or infection, any mites living on its skin can run amok, burrowing through the skin. This leads to hair loss, swelling and redness, itching, scaling, and greasiness on the fur. Whereas mites may be treatable at home, you should take any animals with mange to the vet; a mite infection this severe is a definite sign of other problems under the surface.

Lice and fleas can also affect pet rats. Fleas are most common when they share a household with dogs and cats. Since fleas are so quick to move from host to host, you should treat all the animals in your house once one animal is found to have fleas. Pyrethrin-based flea shampoos for cats work well with rats. Lice can be more difficult to eliminate. Most rats are asymptomatic carriers, meaning they show no signs of illness. Lice are very common in rats bought from pet stores, and can quickly spread to the rest of the cage if they're not treated. Luckily, lice are not cross-species feeders. The lice your rats have can't be transmitted to you, and if your kid gets lice at school, she won't transfer them to the rats. Lice are easy to kill; the eggs are harder to get rid of. Thoroughly clean and disinfect the cage, then continue to treat the infected rats once a week for at least a month to make sure all the nits have been killed.

Rats sometimes get abscesses. These are soft, warm swellings where pus and bacteria has accumulated underneath the skin, and will be very painful for your rat when pressure is applied. These are sometimes caused when an injury gets infected but can also be a sign of malnutrition. Most abscesses will drain on their own. Treat the wound with hydrogen peroxide or a topical antibiotic ointment. If the rat seems otherwise happy and healthy, just keep an eye on him; it shouldn't require any additional treatment. If the rat starts developing signs of illness, or if the abscess won't drain and gets hard, you should call the vet to have it lanced.

Bumblefoot

Ulcerative pododermatis—known colloquially as bumblefoot by pet owners—is an infection of the calluses on the soles of your rats' feet, most often caused by walking on exposed wire flooring. It appears as dark discolored sores on the bottom of the foot. Your first step of treatment should be to cover the offending floor with a piece of cloth or Plexiglas. Bumblefoot is very painful, and you'll see affected rats limping noticeably as they navigate their enclosure. The problem may go away on its own after the issues with the cage have been fixed, but serious cases may require antibiotic treatment from your vet.

Eye problems

Rats may get infections of the eye, the most common of which are conjunctivitis (inflammation of tissue around the eye) and keratitis (inflammation of the cornea). Both ailments are caused by viral or bacterial infections, and cause discharge from the eyes, swelling around the eyes or neck, excessive porphyrin staining, rubbing or scratching at the face, and hair loss. In severe cases, the cornea may turn cloudy or bluish.

One specific strain of viral conjunctivitis is seen most often in rats. Sialodacryoadentitis virus (SDA) affects the saliva and tear production glands, and is sort of like a human's chicken pox—most rats get it, and once they have it once, they'll never get it again. It is highly contagious, but once one rat in your colony gets it, it should run its course through the whole cage in 1-2 months. Your vet can give you antibiotics to treat the infection. The most serious potential problem is a secondary infection by mycoplasma because of the compromised immune system. Young, healthy rats are less at risk for this than rats that are elderly or already debilitated.

Tumors

As rats age, they are prone to developing tumors. Some of these are benign, meaning they don't spread to other organs; others are malignant, spreading throughout the body, especially to the lungs where they cause difficulty breathing. The main issue with benign tumors is that they push other organs aside. They may also grow so large they exceed their blood flow, making the tissue in the tumor die and leading to gangrene, which releases toxic substances into the rat's body. These problems can be fatal, so you should take your rats to the vet to address any tumors.

Mammary tumors are the most common kind in female rats. These occur around the genitals, across the chest, and under the armpits. While 90% of mammary tumors are benign, they can get large and infected and will likely need to be removed. Mammary tumors can be largely prevented by spaying.

Other problems

Problems with the internal organs can be difficult to identify in rats. The symptoms can be similar to respiratory infections, but may also include diarrhea, loss of weight or refusal to eat, or excessive drinking and urination. Again, your best option is to isolate the sick animal and call the vet if symptoms worsen or persist.

Most rats are completely capable of wearing their teeth down on their own, but in rare cases their teeth don't line up right and as a result continue to grow past a healthy length. This is known as malocclusion, and can eventually lead to mouth injuries if left untreated. The teeth can be trimmed down, but it's best to take your pet to the vet to do this so you don't risk fracturing your rat's tooth due to inexperience.

While rats may limp or favor a paw after an injury, you should take your animal to the vet if you notice persistent lameness or strange angles to the limbs. Sudden lack of coordination, partial paralysis, trembling, or seizures accompanying the limp are signs of a more serious problem, and could be caused either by a stroke or issues with the nervous system. Rats over 2 years of age may develop a condition known as degenerative myelopathy, which affects the nerves that carry signals to the muscles. This condition is debilitating but not fatal, and though they may have more issues moving around, a rat can live with myelopathy happily for years with proper care. Your vet can diagnose the issue more accurately and recommend treatment.

If you have young rats, you should keep your eye out for ringtail, especially in the winter months. This infection of the tail is caused by low humidity, and takes the form of ring-like sores and scars around the tail, sometimes causing the end of the tail to fall off. This is most common in unweaned kittens, and you're unlikely to have to worry about it unless you're breeding. The same thing is true of a condition known as megacolon, which is a rarer but significantly more serious issue. Rats with megacolon never develop the nerves that tell their colon when to release waste. They'll experience constipation offset by intense diarrhea and will be sluggish and underweight, with very little appetite and a distended abdomen. Megacolon is an inherited disease that is always fatal. Parents of rats that develop megacolon should not be used again for breeding.

Caring for a sick rat

Hydration is the most important thing for a sick rat in quarantine. You should carefully monitor their water consumption during recovery. If they do get dehydrated, you can use an oral syringe to administer a pediatric electrolyte replacement. If your rat is having trouble eating, you can also use an oral syringe to feed them soft foods, like applesauce, baby food, and yogurt. Ailing rats need more protein than when they're healthy to help bolster their immune system. Give sick rats an extra serving of protein every day.

Seriously ill or underweight animals may benefit from an incubator. You want to carefully monitor the temperature inside the cage if you're using external heating, and make sure it doesn't get above 80°F. If your rat starts to pant, turn off the heat source. You can put a heating pad on the lowest setting under one half of the cage, leaving the other half cooler for the rat to escape the heat if he wants. Thermal Concepts sells a microwaveable device called a Snuggle Safe that you can use to give extra heat to your rats. You can also place a hot water bottle inside the quarantine cage. Never put an immobile rat on top of any heating source. If they can't move away they're at greater risk to overheat, or even to receive thermal burns from extended contact.

Oral medications are the easiest to administer to a rat. It's easier to give these mixed into treats than by putting them on lab blocks—rats are quick to taste changes in their standard food, but their sweet tooth means they'll gobble down treats regardless of what's in them. Mix medicines into applesauce, jam, pureed fruit, or fruit juice. You can also use honey, syrup, or gelatin deserts to medicate your pet rats. You shouldn't put medicine in a rat's drinking water unless you've been explicitly instructed to do so by your vet. The odd taste could mean your pets won't drink at all, leading to dehydration and further complications. Medicating the drinking water is typically only done when an entire large colony needs the same medication.

If your rat has an eye or ear issue that requires topical drops, administration of these medicines can be a bit trickier. Most rats can be immobilized by scruffing. To do this, gently pinch the loose skin at the back of the rat's neck with your thumb and forefinger then lift them up until their feet are suspended in the air. If your rat doesn't respond well to scruffing, you can also immobilize him by wrapping him snugly in a small towel. Lay the towel flat on a table and lay the rat on top of it, with just his head hanging over the edge. Extend the front paws back then wrap the animal snugly in the towel. Make sure you leave the rat enough space to breathe when you do this.

Breeding your rats

Getting rats to mate is not a problem—in fact, quite the opposite: sexually intact males and females kept in the same enclosure are almost guaranteed to mate. Rats are polygamous by nature, though female rats do occasionally show a preference for males they've mated with before (male rats do not have these same standards). Because of this, you have to be very careful when you're breeding to avoid pairing up close family relatives. Experienced breeders may employ selective breeding programs, by which they will mate closely-related animals occasionally in order to bring out certain genetic traits. This is done methodically, with the mating pair's lineage often tracked back several generations. As a home breeder, you should not allow your rat to mate with any of its siblings, parents, or children. Inbred animals live shorter lives, have a lower disease resistance, and may also develop behavioral problems.

Female rats are capable of producing a lot of young in the course of a year. A single litter can contain anywhere from 1-22 kittens, though the average litter is around 6-12. Before undertaking any breeding program, you should be sure to have a plan in mind of what to do with the babies. If you want to keep them, remember that the males will need to be separated from the females shortly after weaning, and that you'll need separate housing for these kittens while you make the introductions to your established rats. A female rat who's about to give birth should also be given her own enclosure. This means a minimum of 4 total full-sized cages for even a single breeding pair—one cage each for the adult males and adult females, and one cage for each gender of young. Consider whether this will be a problem.

The information provided here gives a general overview of good breeding practices, but if you're serious about breeding your animals you should do further research. Talk the issue over with your vet, or see if the breeder you bought your animals from would be willing to give you some tips and advice.

Sexual maturity and breeding cycles

Males and females both tend to enter puberty at around 2 months, though it may take 3-4 months for the rats to become fertile. Females may be capable of bearing young as early as 5 weeks, but you should wait until around 12-15 weeks (3-4 months) to begin breeding your animals. Rats are most fertile between 3 and 10 months of age, with a female rat's menopause starting at around 15 months. A female rat is capable of producing a litter every month, but for the sake of her health, it's not recommended to breed her more frequently than every 2-3 months to make sure she's got time to fully recover between litters.

A female rat enters heat every 4-5 days and will be receptive to male advances for around 12 hours of this cycle. Pregnancy only lasts for about 3 weeks. You can tell your rat's in heat because the other females will respond and attempt to mount her. If you touch her hindquarters, she'll stretch out with her nose in the air and her haunches raised and start to vibrate her ears. Female rats kept in the same enclosure will often end up with their cycles aligned, with all of them going into heat at around the same time. Because of this, it may be best not to simply put the male rat in the female's cage, unless you're ready to handle more than one pregnancy at a time. The neutral space where your rats play may be a better place to do the mating.

If you have multiple male rats, the alpha male will be the most fertile. If you have a pair of males, both may be equally fertile; if you have 5 or more in a cage, the most subservient males will likely show no interest in mating at all, and may even be frightened of a female in heat. Even if you have two fertile males, you will want to only breed with one at a time. Males that get along at other times will almost certainly start to fight when there's a female in heat around. If you want to move your breeding pair into their own enclosure for a couple days while you're breeding, you can do so. Just make sure to return the alpha male to the colony within 2 days so the hierarchy doesn't get disturbed.

Pregnancy

Rat pregnancies last around 21-23 days. The mother won't begin to show until around 14-15 days. If you've witnessed a successful mating, you should assume the female is pregnant and give her extra servings of protein, offering twice the amount of food you would normally give her. You'll know when your female's about to give birth because she'll start building a nest out of her bedding either the day before or the day of labor. Labor typically lasts around 1-2 hours. The kittens, when born, will be hairless, have their eyes shut, and be about the size of grapes.

Raising and weaning

Baby rats rely on their mother completely for the first 3 weeks—they can't even urinate on their own when they're first born. The mother will also be very protective of her young during this time, and will likely bite you if you attempt to touch her babies. As tempting as it may be, never handle newborn rats. A female whose nest is disturbed, in extreme situations, may even destroy the nest and consume or kill the young, and you want to give them plenty of privacy to avoid having this happen.

Don't keep a male with the female while it's caring for a litter. The female is capable of breeding within a couple days of giving birth and may become pregnant again too soon, leaving her body too few nutrients to properly nurse her young. Female rats often share the care of a litter in the wild, and they may also do this in captivity. On the other hand, some females will try to steal the babies and nurse them herself, or kill the babies of another female. Have a secondary enclosure ready to go just in case. If you do need to separate the colony, let the mother and her babies have the main cage, and remove other adult rats temporarily to a new enclosure.

Rat kittens stay with their mother for a minimum of 4 weeks; large litters may be left with the mother up to 5 weeks. By 10 days old, the new kittens should start to grow hair and open their eyes. At around the 3-week mark, they'll start eating the mother's food, and will be completely weaned by 5 weeks at the latest. Nursing mothers and newborn babies should be given the same extra nutrition as a pregnant female— far more protein, and about twice the amount you'd normally give based on weight.

Most litters will be about 40% male and 60% female, though this will obviously vary, and all-female or all-male litters have been witnessed. If both genders are represented, you should separate them when they're between 5-6 weeks old. You shouldn't keep the babies with the mother past 6 weeks; even if you plan on keeping the female rats and want them to eventually share an enclosure, you should remove them by at least 6 weeks of age, and then return them to the main cage when it's time to establish dominance, at around 10 weeks. If you are selling or giving away the rats, you can start to re-home them as soon as they're completely weaned—4 to 6 weeks is an ideal age to give them to new homes.

Chapter 5: Training and Showing

Some people are surprised to learn that rats can be trained to do tricks. Rats are just as intelligent as a dog and are capable of learning to do somewhat complex tasks. They can be trained to fetch, to come when called, or to use a litter box—given enough patience and positive encouragement.

Before you get too excited, it should be noted that there are some thing you can't expect to train a rat to do. A rat can't be truly housebroken, in the sense that it can run around all day and only pee and poop in its litter box. Rats use urine to mark their territory and if you let them run around the house, you should expect they'll pee on the occasional wall, carpet, or couch arm. There are also some natural instincts you can't train out of a rat. You can't train a rat—especially a female—not to explore. They also can't be trained not to chew on things. Even the best-trained rat should be carefully supervised when there are potential hazards nearby (cats aren't the only animals prone to death by curiosity).

The first step to training your rat is to form a strong trust bond. The second step is to buy a lot of treats. Regardless of what you're training the animal to do, what you're actually doing—from a psychological standpoint—is forming an association between an action or sound and a reward. Rats are quick to form those correlations in their mind. Once the association gets formed, they'll continue to perform the action even if they don't get a treat every time. This is what makes training a rat to not do things so difficult. While they will avoid things they don't like, if you yell at them for peeing on the wall, they won't dislike peeing on walls—they'll dislike you, as the source of that discomfort.

The treat you use in training should be a specific item. Figure out some food your rat particularly loves in the first month or so of bonding. It might be a certain flavor of yogurt drops, a certain kind of food—whatever it is, make that food his training treat. Not only will the rat be especially eager to receive this favorite morsel, the taste of the object will take on a certain association in the rat's mind: This taste means my human wants me to learn something, and I'll get more if I figure out what that is.

Litter box training

Litter box training comes with an inherent reward—a clean enclosure. Many rats will naturally use an offered litter box with little to no prodding from you. Occasionally, though, it does take some convincing.

First of all, when you first bring your rats home you should keep the litter box out of the cage for the first few days. Note where the soiled areas of the bedding are during daily cleaning. There will probably be a specific corner—usually one of the ones in the back—that the rats have designated the bathroom. Once you've established where this is, clean the bedding, saving a few pieces of the soiled bedding back. Put these in the litter box, on top of the litter, then put the litter box in the designated bathroom corner. The first few times you notice them using the litter box, give them a treat to let them know they're doing something good. Because you're working with their instinct, this is usually the easiest training to do.

Coming when called

This is the first "trick" you should start with when you're training your rats, because it's the simplest for them to comprehend. It's a one-to-one association—this specific noise translates to reward. This can also work with other sounds, like bells and clickers. If you want the rat to respond to his name, use a single version of that name when you're training him. Pet names, nick-names, and variants can confuse him. It's also best to do the training one-on-one to minimize distractions.

Start by putting the rat in an open area, like a bed or a sofa. Sit on the other side of it and call his name (or click the clicker or ring the bell, if you're using an object). He'll probably ignore you and continue sniffing and exploring; that's fine. Keep calling his name until he eventually wanders over to you. The first time this happens, it will be by pure coincidence. Give him a treat and let him wander off again. Continue the process of calling his name and rewarding him when he comes. Don't reward him if he comes back to you when you didn't call his name, or he'll just start thinking you're a treat machine.

Do this for a few minutes every day. It can take a week or more of steady effort, but soon your rat will come to you the majority of times it hears its name. Once your rat gets to this point, you can switch to a combination of rewards. Sometimes still give him the treats, but other times give him a social reward, like petting him or scratching his head. As the behavior becomes cemented, you can phase out the treats entirely.

Training other tricks

Rats can be trained to do a lot of things, but the basic structure of all of these follows the outline above. The more steps are involved, the harder it will be and the longer it will take. As a general note on training, it's important that your rat enjoys the training for it to be successful. Don't try to do any marathon training sessions—even an eager rat will probably get bored after about 30 minutes of work, and most rats will top out at 15 minutes in a session. Daily reinforcement of good behavior secures it in the animal's mind, and if the rat has fun doing it, he'll want to do it even more.

Once you've taught your rat to come when called, the next easiest tricks will be single actions, like standing up, laying down, or shaking hands. Again, you'll be starting with rewarding a coincidence. To get the rat to stand up, hold the treat just out of reach above his head, forcing him to stand on his back legs to reach it. When he does, say the command and give him the treat. Just like with teaching his name, you want to avoid using any phrasing variants with the command. You can use any word, but make it the same word or sound every time. Say the command while the rat is still standing but before handing over the treat. After you've done this a few times, try reversing the process. Say the command word without holding any treats out. If the rat stands up, reward him. Again, phase out the treats once he seems to be getting the hang of it, switching to social rewards.

To train your rat to shake hands, some physical manipulation of the rat will be required. Sit with the rat close to you and gently extend his paw, touching it to your hand. Say the command when you do this, then give your rat his treat. Repeat the process until he starts putting his paw in your hand on his own.

The process of training to lie down is similar, but requires a slightly different approach. If you just put the treat on the ground, the rat won't necessarily have to lie down to eat it. What you should do, instead, is watch for moments that your rat lays down on its own. When this happens, say the command and give a treat. You can also do this for other natural behaviors, like climbing and jumping, but stick to one at a time to keep the rat from getting confused. Once you've reinforced a behavior with the command word and treat on a few consecutive days, try reversing the process—say the command, and reward the rat if it does what it should.

Once you've gotten your rat to do a few single-action tricks, you can move on to sequential tricks. These are more complicated and time-consuming because you have to break the trick down into each of its components. With the tricks above you weren't really teaching the rat to do anything new, only to perform familiar behaviors at specific times. Teaching a rat an entirely new behavior is more complicated. Let's use teaching a rat to play fetch as an example.

There are four basic steps in this process from the rat's standpoint: Chase the object, pick up the object, carry the object to my human, and release the object. Since we want all of these objects to be included under a single command, don't worry about associating actions with commands until the whole process has been learned. To teach a rat to fetch, you want to use something that they like, but not something that they can eat. A block of wood, scrap of cloth, or favorite small toy should do fine. If you notice them stealing particular objects from you when they're out and about (rubber erasers and bottle caps are often particularly appealing) you can use one of those. The rat obviously wants to take it from you anyway. The real challenge will be getting him to give it back.

Most rats will happily chase an object when it's thrown. Don't throw the object too far, so you can get to him and give him a treat when he picks it up. If he won't chase the object, instead hold it out for him to take, and give him a treat when he picks it up. You can gradually throw the object further and further away as he grasps that he'll be rewarded for grabbing it. Make sure he's mastered this step and is consistently chasing and grabbing objects before moving on to the next phase.

You've already taught your rat to come when called, so once he's chasing and grabbing the object, call his name while he has it in his mouth—but only give him a reward if he brings the object with him (this includes social rewards). If he comes to you but doesn't bring the object, retrieve the object and try again. Like before, you want to make sure he's got this step before moving on, starting with treats to reinforce then gradually shifting into social rewards instead. Some rats very much want their new toy to live in their cage or nest instead of in your hand, and won't bring it back to you even when you call their name. If this happens, you can put a treat in the palm of your hand and make sure the rat can see it. The promise of food should outweigh the desire to hoard and lead the rat straight to you.

Finally, you want the rat to drop the object in your hand. This step often needs to be trained separately from the rest of the process because the rat will not want to give his prize back. Usually if you put a treat in your open palm the rat will decide to drop the object in favor of the treat. You may need to physically intervene, pulling the object gently from the rat's mouth and putting it in your palm. Once the rat is going through the entire process of fetching, you can introduce the command. Say the command after he's completed the entire process, immediately before giving him the treat.

If you want to take fetching to the next level, you can also teach your rat to retrieve specific objects from around the room. To do this, you want to train a rat what different objects are. Like with other commands, do this one object at a time so you don't confuse your pet. Put the object in your training space. The rat will probably investigate it without prompting; when he does, say the name of the object, and give him a treat. Eventually, you should be able to say that object's name and have the rat go to it, knowing this object is a pen, or block, or what have you. Once you've taught the rat two or more objects, try putting them out at the same time, giving him a treat when he goes to the right one. Once he can do this, you can add the fetch command relatively easily. While this should go without saying, don't ask your rat to fetch you anything that will be harmful to it, or that's too heavy for it to carry.

Rat shows

People have been showing rats since the 19th century, but these events have seen a surge in popularity since the 1990s. Similar to dog shows, these events have rats judged on a variety of physical characteristics. While these specific characteristics tend to differ between various rat organizations, a recent push toward standardization may make them more uniform in future shows. If you plan on showing your rat, you can register your pet with the North American Rat Registry. This organization doesn't hold shows of its own, but some groups require rats to be registered through the NARR before appearing.

Make sure your rats are healthy and friendly with strangers before deciding to take them to a show. If your rat is easily stressed out by new smells, a rat show may be overwhelming. Some rats seem to very much enjoy the showing process, but you should always think first about the health and happiness of your animal before deciding to enter him in these kinds of events. It's also important to quarantine any animals you've taken to a show for about 2 weeks afterwards. With so many other rats in one place, you can never be sure what kinds of bacteria and parasites also tagged along for the ride. It's relatively rare for a rat to get sick at a show, but if he does you don't want that ailment to spread to the rest of the colony.

Generally speaking, female rats tend to show better than males. Rats with kinked tails, notched ears, or other flaws are unlikely to show well. Similarly, obese animals are typically penalized, and animals with missing toes or visible tumors may be disqualified. Female rats that are pregnant or just had a litter should not be brought to shows. Make sure your rat is in tip top form if you want him to do well. Give your animal a bath a few days before the show date. On the day of the show, you can use a piece of silk to comb his fur and make sure it's all laying flat.

Finding and preparing for a show

If you live in North America, the American Fancy Rat & Mouse Association has a list of various rat clubs and show dates on their website. If you live in the Northeast or Midwest, you can also check around at Rat Meetups to see if there are any events coming up in your area. Rat owners living in the UK can find shows through the National Fancy Rat Society. This organization is very active and has multiple shows per year.

Rats are shown in designated "show tanks" so that their owner can't be identified and all individuals have a level playing field. You may need to buy this tank before the day of the show, though some organizations also make tanks available to rent. Pay special attention to the specific requirements of housing set by your particular club. Some groups specify certain kinds of bedding, or certain size restrictions or materials for food dishes and water bottles. Typically, you will need a separate show tank for each rat, though same-sex kittens may be able to be shown in a single tank if their appearances are significantly different.

You should also be aware of your particular club's registration deadlines. Some will require you to submit entries before coming to the event, while others will permit registration the day of (though there may be an extra cost associated). Again, it's important to get information about your organizations shows well ahead of time and read this material thoroughly.

What to expect

Most shows start in the late morning and wrap up in the early evening. Judging typically starts early in the day, and if you're showing a rat you want to arrive at least a half an hour before the start of judging time. If you're just going to a rat show to check it out, it's best to wait to arrive until about 30 minutes after judging starts, when things will be less hectic.

You will typically not be charged for entry into a show, and it's usually a good idea to come to one as a spectator to see how things work in this particular organization before bringing your rats along. When you're showing, there's usually a per-animal charge to enter (typically around $2-$5 per entry). Most organizations will require the rats to pass a basic health screening before being allowed to show. If one rat that you bring fails the health inspection, none of your rats will be permitted to show in the event, in case they are asymptomatic carriers of the infection.

Rats are divided into classes based on overall appearance for the show. This may be done by coat color or by variety; recognized varieties of the AFRMA include Standard, Rex, Tailless, Hairless, Satin, Dumbo, and Bristle Coat. The NRFA in the UK doesn't permit the showing of Tailless or Hairless animals, but otherwise recognizes a similar list. Other clubs may have different groupings, but these are the main large organizations and a lot of smaller clubs adopt these standards. There's a broad array of different color categories that your rat might fit into; if you want to learn more about this, you can check out the show class information on the AFRMA website.

Rat shows often will have other events going on, including exhibitions from breeders and supply companies and the sale or adoption of young rats. Even if you don't ever plan on showing your animals, it might be worth it to check out one of these events. You can learn a lot from talking to the other rat enthusiasts you'll meet at the show. If you're in the market for new animals, extra toys, or alternate foods and beddings, the variety you'll see at a rat show can't be matched by any single store or breeder.

Additional Resources

For additional reading, I recommend these internet forums & websites:

- American Fancy Rat & Mouse Association

  http://www.afrma.org

  Their show listing:

http://www.afrma.org/findshows.htm

  Show class information:

http://www.afrma.org/classes.htm

- National Fancy Rat Society (UK)

  http://www.nfrs.org

- North American Rat Registry

  http://www.ratregistry.org

- The Rat and Mouse Club of America

  http://www.rmca.org

  Their vet database:

http://www.rmca.org/vets/index.php?action=list

- The Rat Fan Club http://www.ratfanclub.org/

Their breeder database:

http://www.ratfanclub.org/breeders.html

- Rat Meetups http://rat.meetup.com

- Rat Forum http://www.ratforum.com/

- Fancy Rats (Forum)

  http://www.fancyratsforum.co.uk/

- The Rat Shack (Forum)

  http://www.ratshackforum.com/forum/

Made in the USA
Middletown, DE
12 December 2020